T0114281

Along the Path to
ENLIGHTENMENT

Also by Dr. David R. Hawkins

Healing and Recovery

Reality, Spirituality, and Modern Man

Discovery of the Presence of God

Transcending the Levels of Consciousness

Truth vs. Falsehood

I: Reality and Subjectivity

The Eye of the I

*Power vs. Force**

Orthomolecular Psychiatry (with Linus Pauling)

*Available from Hay House

Please visit:
Hay House USA: **www.hayhouse.com**®
Hay House Australia: **www.hayhouse.com.au**
Hay House UK: **www.hayhouse.co.uk**
Hay House India: **www.hayhouse.co.in**

Along the Path to ENLIGHTENMENT

365 Daily Reflections from
David R. Hawkins, M.D., Ph.D.

Edited by Scott Jeffrey

HAY HOUSE, INC.
Carlsbad, California • New York City
London • Sydney • New Delhi

Library of Congress Control Number: 2010930027

Tradepaper ISBN: 978-1-4019-3113-1
Digital ISBN: 978-1-4019-3114-8

1st edition, February 2011
2nd edition, September 2011

Printed in the United States of America

Student: What statement would summarize a whole life of spiritual experience and dedication?

Teacher: Gloria in Excelsis Deo!
[Glory to God in the Highest!]

CONTENTS

PREFACE

Each step along the way to enlightenment is exciting and rewarding when its essence is revealed. Taken out of context, any critical insight can seem baffling, yet intriguing. For each seeker, there are important key understandings that light the way and facilitate success. This is a collection of such truths that serve as fulcrums for major leaps forward. Although there are many doorways to heaven, each seeker must find his or her own route.

Comprehension at great depths unravels the essential truth of seeming complexity. It is said that there are 10,000 ways to God, yet they can all be reduced to certain critical elements common to all successful pathways. Therefore, each of the accompanying quotes is proven to be of great value.

— Bon voyage!
David R. Hawkins, M.D., Ph.D.

≋ ≋

INTRODUCTION

Students of David R. Hawkins's work have realized that the truths revealed are ideally suited for spiritual aspirants of the Western world. The teachings are both in accord with the greatest mystics throughout history, and immensely practical in their application to daily life. Just one of these quotes or passages can transform a person's life and catapult him or her ahead on the spiritual journey.

The selections herein were chosen to help you focus on a single quote, idea, or passage on a daily basis. No prior experience or exposure to Dr. Hawkins's work is required to extract benefits from these powerful truths. You may wish to challenge yourself to apply the thought to your life circumstances or merely contemplate or hold the quote in mind throughout the day.

Place this book in a convenient location: on your nightstand, on your desk, in your car, or in your handbag or briefcase. Select a set time each day to read the Divine wisdom of Dr. Hawkins's teachings.

Quotes and passages have been handpicked from Dr. Hawkins's writings, including *Power vs. Force; The Eye of the I; I: Reality and Subjectivity; Truth vs. Falsehood; Transcending the Levels of Consciousness; Discovery of the Presence of God;* and *Reality, Spirituality, and Modern Man.* The passages are presented as they are in Dr. Hawkins's original work; only minor alterations have been made where appropriate. (If you find any of the terms used herein to be unfamiliar, please consult the Glossary at the back of the book.)

I leave you with Dr. Hawkins's words from *The Eye of the I:* "At some point, the illusion breaks down and the opening for the start of the spiritual quest commences. The quest turns from without to within, and the search for answers begins."

May you find the answers you seek within. . . .

— Blessings,
Scott Jeffrey

DAILY REFLECTIONS

January 1

Q: *Where does one begin the search for spiritual truth and self-realization called enlightenment?*

A: It is simple. Begin with who and what you are. All truth is found within. Use verified teachings as a guide.

January 2

The world of the ego is like a house of mirrors through which the ego wanders, lost and confused, as it chases the images in one mirror after another. Human life is characterized by endless trials and errors to escape the maze. At times, for many people (and possibly for most), the world of mirrors becomes a house of horrors that gets worse and worse. The only way out of the circuitous wanderings is through the pursuit of spiritual truth.

January 3

All life ebbs and flows. Everyone is born, suffers afflictions, and dies. There is happiness and sadness, catastrophe and success, increase and decrease. The stock market rises and falls. Diseases and accidents come and go. The karmic dance of life unfolds in the karmic theater of the universe.

January 4

To become more conscious is the greatest gift anyone can give to the world; moreover, in a ripple effect, the gift comes back to its source.

January 5

The infinite field of consciousness is All Present, All Powerful, and includes All of Existence. Thus, nothing can possibly happen outside its infinite domain because it is the Source of Existence. Within this infinite field of power, there are decreasing levels of energy fields. As they are expressed progressively in form (linearity), their relative power decreases all the way down to the individual.

The giant field could be compared to an immense electrostatic field in which the individual is like a charged particle that, because of the infinite power of the field, is automatically aligned within the field according to its individual "charge." The charge of the karmic spiritual body is set by intention, decision, and alignment by intention.

It appears to naïve perception that what is not intellectually explicable seems to be "accidental," especially when the event is unpredictable. Inasmuch as the infinite field of consciousness is unlimited in dimension, nothing can happen outside of it. All that occurs within it is under its influence, and therefore, nothing "accidental" is possible in reality.

January 6

The goal of society in general is to succeed in the world, whereas the goal of enlightenment is to transcend beyond it.

January 7

By inner humility plus wisdom, the seeker of truth takes serious note of the inherent limitations of the human psyche itself and no longer relies on the impressionable personal ego as its sole arbiter of truth.

January 8

Spiritual development is not an accomplishment but a way of life. It is an orientation that brings its own rewards, and what is important is the direction of one's motives.

January 9

To merely hear a great teaching is itself the consequence of spiritual merit. To act on it is of even greater benefit.

January 10

Q: What can we actually do to be helpful to the world?

A: Make a gift of your life and lift all mankind by being kind, considerate, forgiving, and compassionate at all times, in all places, and under all conditions, with everyone as well as yourself. That is the greatest gift anyone can give.

January 11

Spiritual learning does not occur in a linear progression like logic. It is more that familiarity with spiritual principles and disciplines opens awareness and self-realization. Nothing "new" is learned; instead, what already exists presents itself as completely obvious.

January 12

All spiritual truth is contained in every spiritual concept. It is only necessary to completely and totally understand *one single concept* to understand all of them in order to arrive at the realization of the Real.

January 13

All avenues of questioning lead to the same ultimate answer. The discovery that nothing is hidden and truth stands everywhere revealed is the key to enlightenment about the simplest practical affairs and the destiny of mankind. In the process of examining our everyday lives, we can find that all our fears have been based on falsehood. The displacement of the false by the true is the essence of the healing of all things visible and invisible.

January 14

Classically, the readiness for serious spiritual work is referred to as "ripeness," at which point even hearing a single word, phrase, or name may trigger a sudden decision and commitment to truth. The advent of spiritual dedication may thus be subtle, slow, and gradual, and then take a very sudden and major jump. By whatever route, once the seed falls on ready ground, the journey begins in earnest. Commonly, the turning point can be triggered by an unexpected flash of insight, and from that moment on, life changes.

January 15

Out of all-inclusive, unconditional compassion comes the healing of all mankind.

January 16

In a universe where "like goes to like" and "birds of a feather fly together," we attract to us that which we emanate.

January 17

The will is activated and empowered by devotion, and it responds with inspiration, which leads to illumination by grace. The personal will dissolves into Divine Will, and the spark that leads to the spiritual search and inquiry is a Divine gift.

January 18

Every act or decision we make that supports life supports *all* life, including our own. The ripples we create return to us.

January 19

Everything in the universe constantly gives off an identifiable energy pattern of a specific frequency that remains for all time and can be read by those who know how. Every word, deed, and intention creates a permanent record; every thought is known and recorded forever. There are no secrets; nothing is hidden, nor can it be. Everyone lives in the public domain. Our spirits stand naked in time for all to see. Everyone's life, finally, is accountable to the universe.

January 20

Q: What should be the overall context of spiritual endeavor?

A: Selfless service out of love for all creatures and creation. To pursue enlightenment serves God and fellow humans. Be alert and attuned to the innate beauty of all that exists. See the charm and quaintness of even what the world would consider old, beat-up, and ugly.

January 21

It could be said that truth and reality represent an equivalence, and the validity of that equivalence can now be verified by reference to a calibrated scale of levels of truth that are objective, impersonal, and independent of the opinion of the observer. It is important to realize that *a statement of an alleged truth requires specification of context.*

January 22

One basic principle has the power to resolve the problems of the social marketplace: *Support the solution instead of attacking the supposed causes.*

January 23

Humanity is an "affliction" we're all burdened with. We don't remember asking to be born, and we subsequently inherited a mind so limited it is hardly capable of distinguishing what enhances life from what leads to death. The whole struggle of life is in transcending this myopia.

January 24

The living proof of God's love and will for you is the gift of your own existence.

January 25

Life itself has no opinion; it just is. Life effortlessly diverts quickly from one form to another without innate reaction or resistance. It does not even register a reaction to change of form. Life, like light, is innately formless and beyond preference, resistance, or reaction.

January 26

The human world represents a purgatorial-like range of opportunities and choices, from the most grim to the exalted, from criminality to nobility, from fear to courage, from despair to hope, and from greed to charity. Thus, if the purpose of the human experience is to evolve, then this world is perfect just as it is.

January 27

Life unfolds of its own and does not need commentary. The habit of editorializing about what is witnessed needs to be voluntarily surrendered to God.

January 28

Although the human mind likes to believe that it is "of course" dedicated to truth, in reality, what it really seeks is confirmation of what it already believes. The ego is innately prideful and does not welcome the revelation that much of its beliefs are merely perceptual illusions.

January 29

Dedication to truth itself is the rapid road to its discovery.

January 30

The mature spiritual aspirant is one who has explored the ego's options and false promises of happiness.

January 31

Do not compare yourself with others regarding "holiness," merit, goodness, deservingness, sinlessness, and so on. These are all human notions, and God is not limited by human notions.

February 1

In truth, we exist and survive, not because of the ego, but in spite of it.

February 2

Q: *Where is the reality of eternal truth to be found?*

A: Begin by accepting the very important statement that all truth is subjective. Do not waste lifetimes looking for an objective truth because no such thing exists. Even if it did, it could not be found except by the purely subjective experience of it. All knowledge and wisdom are subjective. Nothing can be said to exist unless it is subjectively experienced.

February 3

To best serve the world, seek enlightenment and transcend illusions rather than contribute to them.

February 4

The capacity to recognize the truth is a potential within human consciousness, and the combined intention of the consciousness of all people in that direction intensifies the overall field. At some intuitive level, everyone knows that truth supports life and falsity brings death.

February 5

Human progress is evolutionary, and therefore, mistakes and errors are inevitable. The only real tragedy is to become older but not wiser.

February 6

Acceptance is the great healer of strife, conflict, and upset. It also corrects major imbalances of perception and precludes the dominance of negative feelings. Everything serves a purpose. Humility means that we will not understand all events or occurrences. Acceptance is not passivity, but non-positionality.

February 7

To even hear of enlightenment is already the rarest of gifts. Anyone who has ever heard of enlightenment will never be satisfied with anything else.

February 8

The benefit of accepting one's defects instead of denying them is an increase in an inner sense of self-honesty, security, and higher self-esteem, accompanied by greatly diminished defensiveness. A self-honest person is not prone to having his or her feelings hurt by others; therefore, honest insight has an immediate benefit in the reduction of actual, as well as potential, emotional pain.

February 9

Realize that the depiction of God as a "judge" is a delusion of the ego that arises as a projection of guilt from the punishment of childhood. Realize that God is not a parent.

February 10

How best to "serve the highest good" is in accordance with the prevailing level of consciousness of the observer. There is no single answer for everyone.

February 11

Spiritual progress ensues automatically from choosing good-will, forgiveness, and lovingness as a way of being in the world at large rather than viewing it as a gain-seeking transaction.

February 12

Spiritual evolution is the automatic consequence of watching the mind—and its proclivities as an "it"—from the general view-point of the paradigm of context rather than content. Instead of trying to force change, it is merely necessary to allow Divinity to do so by deeply surrendering all control, resistance, and illusions of gain or loss. It is not necessary to destroy or attack illusions but merely to allow them to fall away.

February 13

To transcend the world requires compassion and acceptance, the result of inner humility, by which the world is surrendered to God with increased peace of mind.

February 14

It is not the world that is a trap, but one's attachment to it, along with one's observations that cloud the search for Truth.

February 15

Attachment is a very peculiar quality of the ego. It can be totally undone in all of its pervasive and multitudinous forms of clinging by simply letting go of one's faith in it, or belief in its value as a reality. The attachment to "self" or "me" or "I" is a basic trap. One can seek out its fantasy value—the self gets attached to what it values.

Note that attachment requires and is sustained by an energy and an intention. The mind is attached to the very process of attachment itself as a survival tool. Letting go of the ego is based on the willingness to surrender attachment to it as a substitute for God.

February 16

What the ego cannot lift with all its might is like a feather to the grace of God.

February 17

The best attitude is one of devotion to truth rather than being contentious toward falsehood. Open-minded curiosity leads to progressive discovery of information never before available, which may therefore seem confrontational upon first exposure.

February 18

Appearance is not essence, perception is not reality, and the cover is not the book. Error is quite often convincing, which is an unpleasant fact to consider and accept. Everyone secretly believes that his or her own personal view of the world is real, factual, and true.

February 19

Spiritual progress is based on acceptance as a matter of free will and choice, and thus everyone experiences only the world of his or her own choosing. The universe is totally free of victims, and all eventualities are the unfolding of inner choices and decisions.

February 20

The less the "wants" prevail, the greater the experience of freedom.

February 21

It is helpful to remember that value and attraction are in the eye of the beholder and are not qualities of the world itself. What is imagined to be "out there" stems from "in here." The same applies to cherished positionalities and seductive presumptions. There are no temptations "out there," and their attraction diminishes by simple refusal and renunciation.

February 22

Accept that the concept of "the fear of God" is ignorance. God is peace and love, and nothing else.

February 23

Traditionally, the pathways to God have been through the heart (love, devotion, selfless service, surrender, worship, and adoration) or through the mind (*Advaita,* or the pathway of nonduality). Each way may seem more comfortable at one stage or another, or they alternate in emphasis.

Whether you take the pathway of the heart or the mind, it is a hindrance to consider that there is a personal self or an "I" or an ego that is doing the striving or seeking or which will become enlightened. It is much easier to realize there is no such thing as the ego or an "I" identity that is doing any seeking; instead, it is an impersonal aspect of consciousness that is doing the exploring and seeking.

February 24

To strive to know God is in itself pristine and the ultimate aspiration.

February 25

A useful approach is to let the love for God replace the willfulness that is driving the seeking. One can release all desire to seek, and realize that the thought that there is anything else but God is a baseless vanity. This is the same vanity that claims authorship for one's experiences, thoughts, and actions. With reflection, it can be seen that both the body and the mind are the result of the innumerable conditions of the universe, and that one is at best the witness of this concordance.

Out of an unrestricted love for God arises the willingness to surrender all motives except to serve God completely. To be the servant of God becomes one's goal rather than enlightenment. To be a perfect channel for God's love is to surrender completely and to eliminate the goal seeking of the spiritual ego. Joy itself becomes the initiator of further spiritual work.

February 26

One is not "forced" to feel resentment by a negative memory, nor does one have to buy into a fearful thought about the future. These are only options. The mind is like a television set running its various channels for selection, and one does not have to follow any particular temptation of thought. One can fall into the temptation of feeling sorry for oneself, or feeling angry or worried. The secret attraction of all these options is that they offer an inner payoff or a secret satisfaction that is the source of the attraction of the mind's thoughts.

February 27

Within limits, we tend to experience the reflection of what we have become.

February 28

The source of joy is always present, always available, and not dependent on circumstances. There are only two obstacles: (1) the ignorance that it is always available and present; and (2) valuing something other than peace and joy above that peace and joy because of the secret pleasure of the payoff.

(BONUS REFLECTION FOR LEAP YEAR DAY)

February 29

The teeth of spiritual work occur when we are confronted with that which we cannot avoid. It is the direct confrontation that requires a leap in consciousness.

March 1

The experience of the presence of God is available and within at all times, but awaits choice. That choice is made only by surrendering everything other than peace and love to God. In return, the Divinity of the Self reveals Itself as ever present—but not experienced—because it has been ignored or forgotten, or one has chosen otherwise.

March 2

Q: What characteristics facilitate comprehension and transformation?

A: Dedication, devotion, faith, prayer, surrender, and inspiration. When the barriers are relinquished, Truth reveals itself spontaneously.

March 3

Disruption of life by the unexpected also creates anxiety at the forced readjustment, which may require major decision making. It is important to know that spiritual research indicates that all suffering and emotional pain result from resistance. Its cure is via surrender and acceptance, which relieve the pain.

March 4

The realization that there is a source of joy and happiness that is beyond the ego is a major step. Then curiosity and an interest in how to reach spiritual goals arises. Belief also arises, which is then bolstered by faith, and eventually by experience. Next follows the acquisition of instruction, information, and the practice of what has been learned. By invitation, the spiritual energy increases, followed by dedication and the willingness to surrender all obstacles.

Even the decision to turn one's life over to God brings joy and gives life a whole new meaning. It becomes uplifting, and the greater context gives life more significance and reward. One eventually becomes unwilling to support negativity, within or without. This is not because it is wrong, but merely futile. Although the journey to God begins with failure and doubt, it progresses into certainty. The way is really quite simple.

March 5

To win in life means to give up the obsession of "who's at fault." Graciousness is far more powerful than belligerence. It is better to succeed than to win.

March 6

By its nature, the pathway to God is not easy. It requires considerable courage, fortitude, willingness, and forbearance. It is strengthened by humility and a benign conscience.

March 7

An extremely valuable insight that is learned by all spiritually evolved persons in the course of their development is seeing one's own personal consciousness as the decisive influence that determines all that occurs in one's life.

March 8

Holding a goal in mind is inspirational and actually helpful to its accomplishment, because what is held in mind tends to actualize. However, it is a mistake to attack oneself with guilt for failing to achieve the ideal. Upon examination, it will be frequently discovered that it was not really the goal that was desired, but the satisfaction that was associated with it.

March 9

Effective spiritual endeavor is a consequence of constancy and persistence rather than fits and starts of enthusiasm.

March 10

Inner satisfaction becomes more important than worldly gain or the desire to control or influence others. Attraction replaces promotion. Eventually, resistance is no longer related to worldly life and its perceived values. Instead, the inner intention is one of purity and selflessness. Thus, evolution becomes the consequence of the process itself rather than a consequence of "seekingness" or acquisition.

March 11

Along the spiritual pathway, blocks and temptations appear, as do doubts and fears. Classically, they have been termed the "tests" that arise from the ego, which does not relish relinquishment of dominion. These are overcome by reaffirmation of goals and commitment, as well as by reinforcing counterbalancing principles such as dedication, tenacity, constancy, courage, conviction, and intention. The greater the challenge, the greater the development of inner strength, decision, and determination. By persistence and discipline, it can be seen that temptation is an option to merely refuse rather than an impulse that calls for attack or negation.

March 12

Attachments are illusions. They can be surrendered out of one's love for God, which inspires the willingness to let go of that which is comfortably familiar.

March 13

Subjectively, all that is needed to progress are patience, prayer, faith in the process, and the surrendering of resistance. Confusion, like a change in the weather, is a transitional condition that clears with patience and also with emergence into the next stage, whereby the confusing condition is transcended.

March 14

It's pleasing to discover that it isn't necessary to drive oneself forward; instead, one can simply allow oneself to move forward as blocks are removed. Thus, one becomes attracted by the future rather than propelled by the past.

March 15

With spiritual maturity, one understands that this lifetime is precious and too valuable to waste on the ideas of being superior or other ego-inflating, vainglorious illusions.

March 16

The best defense against the development of anger is to see others as equals, lessen expectations, and, via humility, surrender the fulfillment of one's wants to God. With progressive detachment and relinquishment of the ego's demands and expectations, anger diminishes.

March 17

One does not become a success by envying and vilifying success, but by imitating it. Thus, the angry person has to go back and make up for what was missing in his or her own education and development.

March 18

There is no art without love. Art is always the making of the soul, the craft of man's touch, whether that touch is corporeal or the touch of the mind and spirit—so it has been since Neanderthal times, and so it will always be.

March 19

True asceticism is simply a matter of economy of effort. It is not possessions themselves but the presumed importance or value projected onto them that is significant. Therefore, it is recommended that one "wear the world like a loose garment."

March 20

Frustration results from exaggerating the importance of desires.

March 21

Awareness of the overall silent contextual field is facilitated by a contemplative lifestyle that could be likened to shifting interest from details to "the big picture." It "gets" overall qualities of atmosphere without going into specifics, and therefore intuits generalities rather than thinking or analyzing.

The resistance of the ego/mind is that it is afraid it might "miss" something, as it is addicted to processing the details of the content of form, which is the attraction and lure of the world. To "renounce the world" means to withdraw energy from it and decline activities that require attention to specifics, thereby abiding in the Self rather than in the amusements of the self.

March 22

We witness, observe, and record apparent processions of experience. But even in awareness itself, nothing actually happens. Awareness merely registers what is being experienced; it has no effect on it. Awareness is the all-encompassing attractor field of unlimited power identical with life itself. *And there is nothing the mind believes that is not erroneous at a higher level of awareness.*

March 23

The process of creativity and genius is inherent in human consciousness. As every human has within himself the same essence of consciousness, so is genius a potential that resides within everyone. It simply waits for the right circumstance to express itself.

March 24

The processing out of anger requires inner honesty and the willingness to surrender what is lacking integrity and essentially unworkable, and replace it with self-confidence. Compensatory attitudes that are far more powerful than anger are dedication, reason, humility, gratitude, perseverance, and tolerance.

March 25

Everyone already at a certain level knows that they "are"; the ego then quibbles about the details of definition, but the Self is not fooled by the ruse. All false identifications can be dropped in an instant with the willingness to surrender all "mentalizations" to God.

March 26

The mind is caught between desires and aversions, both of which are binding. An aversion is also innately an attachment to a conditional perception, and it is disassembled by acceptance.

March 27

All the mind's statements are provisional at best, and an awareness of that limitation is an intrinsic quality of wisdom. Wisdom denotes a degree of humility as well as flexibility. It also implies a conservative, cautious attitude that is aware that further information will accrue over time and experience. Thus, wisdom considers all knowledge to be provisional and subject to change, not only in meaning but also in significance and value.

March 28

All things are self-created by Divine expression as existence. Therefore, each "thing" can only be what it is because of the totality of the entire universe.

March 29

The dualistic mind sees what appears to be an event, a happening, or a thing and hypothesizes another concept, that of "change." The mind seeks explanations and is naïve as to its own structure, motivations, and limitations. In language, it is said that the "I" or an "it" caused a "that," much like that which is intrinsic to sentence structure in which a subject acts on an object via a verb. The self then presumes that there is an inner primary causal agent, such as the "doer" of deeds, the "thinker" of thoughts, and the "deciders" of decisions. Without such a dualistic explanation, the linear mind is at a loss to explain the appearance of phenomena.

March 30

Spiritual work involves withdrawing attachment to, or identification with, content—and then progressively realizing that one's reality is context. The briefest explanation is that the self is content and the Self is context.

March 31

The destiny of the spirit will be, for better or worse, depending on the choices and decisions one makes.

April 1

The level of consciousness is determined by the choices made by the spiritual will, and therefore is the consequence as well as the determinant of karma. Freedom to evolve requires a world that affords the greatest opportunity to ascend or descend the spiritual ladder. Viewed from that perspective, this is an ideal world, and its society is constituted by a wide range of experiential options.

April 2

Until one acknowledges the intrinsic genius within oneself, one will have great difficulty recognizing it in others—we can only acknowledge *without* what we realize *within*.

April 3

One's range of choice is ordinarily limited only by one's vision.

April 4

Freedom is the opportunity to fashion one's own destiny and learn the inherent spiritual truths that are essential. For merit or demerit to occur, the choices have to be made in a state of belief and experience to be considered "real." Thus, even illusion subserves spiritual growth, for it seems real at the time.

April 5

To consistently choose love, peace, or forgiveness leads one out of the house of mirrors.

April 6

Human life subserves the spirit. The world is less painful to witness if it is appreciated as the ultimate school wherein we earn salvation and serve each other through our own lives.

April 7

Awareness is a quality of consciousness itself that is not encumbered by having to "do" anything. It just "is," and by virtue of its innate capacity, apprehends essence directly. The presence of Divinity as Self is effortless.

April 8

Actions are the automatic consequence of the integration of context, field, and intention. All action is actually spontaneous and reflects karmic propensities and local conditions that may or may not favor expression. To depersonalize actions, it is only necessary to let go of the belief that there is a separate, independent causal agent called "I" or "me."

April 9

Actualization is an option and a choice as an aspect of the will. Each positive choice increases the likelihood and probability of additional positive choices. Each positive choice moves one closer to a higher attractor field of consciousness.

April 10

Q: How should one envision spiritual work?

A: The process is one of discovery and is thus directed within. It is by influence of the Self that spiritual endeavor becomes chosen as a life goal. It is primarily a decision.

April 11

As the ego's dominance of perception recedes, so does the appearance of the world and the mind's interpretations. Decisions are based on projected perceptions. Thus, the mind perceives endless illusions, including classifications based on judgments. Those that are interpreted as "good" options are attractive to choice and agreement. Therefore, all perceptions reflect content.

April 12

Commitment is to the core of truth itself and is free of seduction by proselytization or secrecies. All that is necessary is curiosity and an attraction to truth, which is complete, total, and self-sufficient.

April 13

Objectively, it can be seen that thoughts really belong to the consciousness of the world; the individual mind merely processes them in new combinations and permutations. What seem to be truly original thoughts appear only through the medium of genius and are invariably felt by their authors to be a gift, found or given, not self-created. It may be the case that we're each unique, as no two snowflakes are alike . . . however, *we're still just snowflakes.*

April 14

There is no inner "thinker" behind thoughts, no "doer" behind actions, no "seeker" of enlightenment. Seeking occurs on its own when the time is right, and it emerges as a focus of attention. All aspects and qualities of consciousness are self-actuating and energize each other under the general direction of the will.

April 15

In Reality, everything occurs of its own, with no exterior cause. Every thing and every event is a manifestation of the totality of All That Is, just as it is at any given moment. Once seen in its totality, everything is perfect at all times, and nothing needs an external cause to change it in any way. From the viewpoint of the ego's positionality and limited scope, the world seems to need endless fixing and correction. This illusion collapses as a vanity.

April 16

Nothing in the universe happens by chance or accident. The universe is a coherent concurrence and interaction of innumerable conditions attendant on the infinite number of energy patterns. In the state of awareness, all this is obvious and can be clearly seen and known. Outside that level of awareness, it could be likened to innumerable, invisible magnetic fields that automatically coalesce or repel one's position, and which interact according to the positions and relative strengths and polarities. Everything influences everything else and is in perfect balance.

April 17

When one realizes that one is the universe, complete and at one with All That Is, forever without end, no further suffering is possible.

April 18

By observation, it can be seen that beneath the images and words themselves, there is a driving energy, a desire to think, to keep busy with any input the mind can find to fill in the gaps. One can detect a drive to "thinkingness" that is *impersonal*. With observation, one can detect that there is no "I" thinking the thoughts at all. In fact, the "I" rarely intervenes.

April 19

What is searching for higher truth is not a personal "I" but an aspect of consciousness itself, which expresses as inspiration, devotion, dedication, and perseverance—all of which are aspects of the spiritual will. Therefore, the source of the search for the Self is the Self itself actualizing the necessary processes by virtue of its own qualities, which are facilitated by Grace.

April 20

Like springtime, the promise of a new era in man's understanding of God is emerging. Now the level of consciousness of mankind is high enough to be able to recognize the truth of a God of Love instead of worshipping the god of guilt and hate.

April 21

All "problems" are products of mental processing only and do not exist in the world.

April 22

In Reality, everything is automatically manifesting the inherent destiny of its essence; it doesn't need any external help to do this. With humility, one can relinquish the ego's self-appointed role as savior of the world and surrender it straight to God. The world that the ego pictures is a projection of its own illusions and arbitrary positionalities. No such world exists.

April 23

Q: *Is a contemplative lifestyle possible in today's world?*

A: With strong intention, daily life conforms. Contemplation implies nonattachment, which does not preclude activity.

April 24

True happiness is always in the "right now" of this moment. The ego is always anticipating completion and satisfaction in the future "when" a desire gets fulfilled.

April 25

All fields of human knowledge change over time, and even the reporting of history itself is subject to revision based on new discoveries and methodologies. Thus, all beliefs and information are tentative in that even if the facts don't change, their significance or meaning is subject to change over time.

April 26

People with adequate self-esteem have no need to hate others.

April 27

Like a cork in water or a balloon in the atmosphere, each spirit rises to its own level of buoyancy within the infinite realms of energy fields of consciousness. No external "judgment" or Divine coercion is involved. Each being radiates forth its essence and so determines its own destiny. Thus is Divine justice perfect. By choice, each spirit becomes what it has chosen. Within all realms, there exists the moment-to-moment choice of the absolute reality that is ever present and whose absolute choice results in liberation.

April 28

In this interconnected universe, every improvement we make in our private world improves the world at large for everyone. We all float on the collective level of consciousness of mankind so that any increment we add comes back to us. We all add to our common buoyancy by our efforts to benefit life. What we do to serve life automatically benefits all of us because we are all included in that which is life. We *are* life. It's a scientific fact that "what is good for you is good for me."

April 29

A question cannot be asked unless there is already the potentiality of the answer.

April 30

The major limitation of consciousness is its innocence. Consciousness is gullible; it believes everything it hears. Consciousness is like hardware that will play back any software that's put into it. We never lose the innocence of our own consciousness; it persists, naïve and trusting, like an impressionable child. Its only guardian is a discerning awareness that scrutinizes the incoming program.

May 1

Independent of content, the capacity to be, to know, to exist, and to be aware are the *a priori* substrates to life in its expression as consciousness. To exist and be conscious of existence supersedes all logic, reason, or proof. Awareness is aware that it is aware. To know God, it is only necessary to know and fully comprehend the significance that one exists.

May 2

An analysis of the nature of consciousness reveals that redemption occurs as the result of the return of consciousness to its original pristine state of nonduality. It can do so only by the "obedience" of surrendering the dualities of will and willfulness of the ego to the nonduality of God's Truth. The return from the duality of the ego to the nonduality of the spirit is so difficult and unlikely that only by Divine Grace is it even possible. Thus, man needs a savior to be his advocate, his inspiration, and the fulcrum of his salvation from the pain and suffering of the ego.

May 3

Q: *What does "surrender to God" really mean?*

A: It means to surrender control and the secret satisfactions of the ego's positionalities. Turn only to love and to God as the source of life and joy. This choice is available in every instant. When finally chosen, the reward is great. By invitation, spiritual awareness illuminates the way. The key is willingness.

May 4

To surrender what one thinks one is to God does not leave one as "nothing," but quite the contrary: it leads to the discovery that one is everything.

May 5

In and of itself, anger is merely a subjective emotion that does not actually accomplish anything in the world, as the use of reason and restraint would. Anger is used by the ego as a substitute for courage, which really only requires being resolute, determined, or committed.

May 6

Whereas the goal of the ego/mind is primarily to do, act, acquire, or perform, the intention of contemplation is to "become." While the intellect wants to know "about," contemplation seeks knowingness itself and autonomous wisdom. Rational thinking is time related, sequential, and linear. Contemplation, in contrast, occurs outside of sequential time—it is nonlinear and related to comprehension of essence. Devotional contemplation is a way or style of being in the world whereby one's life becomes a prayer.

May 7

Spiritual progress occurs in stages: In the beginning, one learns of spiritual realities and studies them. Then comes the practice and application of the teachings in every aspect of life, and eventually one becomes the prayer. Through devotion, commitment, and practice, spiritual concepts become experiential realities.

May 8

That which manifests and is then said to exist is knowable by virtue of awareness alone, which is that quality of consciousness that allows the knowledge, experience, and awareness that one exists or that one *is*. To *be* is one thing, but to *know that you are* is another.

May 9

Serious inner spiritual work may sound tedious and demanding (to the ego), but is exciting to the spirit, which is eager to return home. Consciousness innately seeks its source.

May 10

The most important element in facilitating an upward movement in consciousness is an attitude of *willingness,* which opens up the mind through new means of appraisal to the possible validity of new hypotheses. Although motives for change are as multitudinous as the innumerable facets of the human condition, they are most often found to arise spontaneously when the mind is challenged in the face of a puzzle or a paradox. In fact, certain disciplines (such as Zen) deliberately create such an impasse in order to finesse a leap of awareness.

May 11

To contribute to the welfare and happiness of others is gratifying and leads to the discovery that generosity is its own reward.

May 12

All mental (linear) depictions of spiritual/religious truth are subject to invalidation, argument, and dispute. In contrast, consciousness itself (nonlinear) is beyond definition or description, and thus not subject to skepticism, doubt, or disbelief.

May 13

As spiritual awareness advances, the flow of spiritual energy increases and enables transcending prior, seemingly insurmountable obstacles. As the attractions of the world and emotions decrease, there is a progressive attraction to qualities such as beauty, lovability, and peace, rather than "things" or seeming gains. Forgiveness becomes a habitual attitude, and the innate innocence of all creation shines forth. The teachings of great saints and teachers become one's own from within.

May 14

Spiritual commitment is energized by the alignment of the spiritual will with the attributes of Divinity, which are truth, love, compassion, wisdom, and nonpartiality. Devotion prioritizes one's life and attracts that which is of assistance. To be a servant of God is a dedication whereby the goal takes precedence over all other positionalities, attractions, or distractions.

May 15

Without consciousness, there would be nothing to experience form. It could also be said that form itself—as a product of perception with no independent existence—is thus transitory and limited, whereas consciousness is all-encompassing and unlimited. How could that which is transitory (with a clear beginning and ending), create that which is formless (all encompassing and unlimited)? However, if we see that the notion of limitation itself is merely a product of perception with no intrinsic reality, then the riddle solves itself: form becomes an expression of the formless.

May 16

We influence others by what we are rather than by what we say or have.

May 17

When examined as a function of the ego, opinion reveals itself to be nothing more than an idea to which self-importance has been added because it is "my" opinion. An opinion is an idea that has acquired the glamour of self-importance and is therefore more attractive than just reason, logic, or facts.

May 18

Although inherent to consciousness itself, context is usually not stated, identified, or defined. Therefore, there has previously been no actual science of truth itself, much less a means of verification or confirmation. So it is inevitable that humanity flounders and repetitively falls into endless disasters (such as repeating the same mistake over and over, hoping for a different result).

May 19

God's grace could be understood as the absolute certainty of the karmic coherence of the entire universe in all its expressions as realms and possibilities. Grace is the provision within the realm of consciousness, for the availability to use all the means to salvation and absolute freedom. By choice, one determines one's own fate. There are no arbitrary forces to be reckoned with.

May 20

In gratitude for the gift of life, one dedicates that life back as a gift to God through selfless service to His creation as all of life.

May 21

That which has existence is already total and complete or it would not exist. Existence does not require dependence on some other condition. Conditional existence is therefore an illusion of the ego/mind, which believes that nothing exists except as dependent on something outside itself. Existence is self-complete and unconditional. Existence is solely by the grace of God, by Divine ordinance.

May 22

If the essential dynamic of one's spiritual seeking is not spiritual ambition (to get somewhere) but the progressive surrender of the obstacles to love, then that which is called "spiritual ego" doesn't arise as an obstacle later.

May 23

Q: *How can one prevent the development of a spiritual ego? Each success seems like it would feed it.*

A: Realize that there is no such entity as the doer of deeds or actions. There is no doer/self to take blame or credit. Progress is the result of a quality of consciousness that has been activated by the assent of the spiritual will. Spiritual inspiration becomes the energy that is operating; it doesn't emanate from the ego/self.

May 24

Emotion is not an indicator of truth, as it is both reflective and determinative of positionalities and conditioning.

May 25

Q: *What is the most serviceable presumptive view of the world for a spiritual student/devotee/seeker?*

A: Presume that the world's actual "purpose" is perfect and fully known only by God. See it as neutral overall, but with the benefit that it provides optimal opportunity for spiritual growth and the evolution of consciousness. It is a school for enlightenment and the revelation of Divinity, whereby consciousness/ awareness reawakens to its source. Thus, to pursue enlightenment in and of itself serves the world and God.

May 26

True generosity expects no reward, for there are no strings attached.

May 27

A self-honest person is not prone to having his or her feelings hurt or "having a bone to pick" with others. Honest insight has an immediate benefit in the reduction of actual as well as potential emotional pain. A person is vulnerable to emotional pain in exact relationship to the degree of self-awareness and self-acceptance.

May 28

The key to painless growth is humility, which amounts to merely dropping pridefulness and pretense, and accepting fallibility as a normal human characteristic of self and others.

May 29

It is of great value to select a basic dictum to live by, such as the decision to be kind and of goodwill toward all life in all its expressions.

May 30

It is helpful to remember that neither truth nor enlightenment is something to be found, sought, acquired, gained, or possessed. The Infinite Presence is always present, and its realization occurs of itself when the obstacles to that realization are removed. It is, therefore, not necessary to study the truth, but only to let go of that which is fallacious. Moving away the clouds does not cause the sun to shine, but merely reveals what was hidden all along.

Spiritual work, in other words, is primarily a letting go of the presumably known for the unknown, with the promise by others who have done it that the effort is more than well rewarded at the end.

May 31

Selecting a basic spiritual dictum to live by operationally becomes a set of attitudes that change perception. It is a style of positioning oneself and relating to life rather than a set of linear belief systems. Attitudes tend to generalize as discernment rather than definable perception.

June 1

The decisions to "be kind to all of life" or to respect the sacredness of all that exists are powerful attitudes in spiritual evolution, along with the virtues of compassion, the willingness to forgive, and seeking to understand rather than to judge. By constantly surrendering, perceptions dissolve into the discernment of essence.

June 2

Judgmentalism is the great vanity of all egos. Scripture says, "Judge not, lest ye be judged." Also, "*Judgment is mine,* sayeth the Lord." Christ said to forgive. The Buddha said that there is nothing to judge because perception can only see illusion. Perception is always partial and limited by an arbitrary context. In truth, no judgment is possible.

June 3

Q: *What about Judgment Day?*

A: Man extrapolates the ego's qualities to God and then fears God. Judgment Day is every day; it is already here and is constant and unending.

June 4

While it is obvious that there are many elements and forces in the world that are deleterious to human life and happiness, it isn't necessary to hate or demonize them—instead, merely make appropriate allowances and avoid them.

June 5

By observation, one will see that the good/bad dichotomy is merely the reflection of an overall contextualization based on unexamined presumptions. With deep humility, one will soon realize that unaided, the mind is really unauthorized, ill equipped, and incapable of making such judgmental discernment. It can make this discovery by just beginning to ask for whom is it good, for whom is it bad, when, and under what circumstances. This eventually leads to examining one's overall contextualization of the significance and meaning of human life itself as a transitional learning experience.

June 6

It is unrealistic as well as eventually injurious to believe that other people "should" adopt and live by one's own personal standards, morals, and code of conduct as well as interpretation of reality. Projected moralism is always expressed as "should" and often leads to resentment, hatred, grudges, or even retaliatory vengeance—and, of course, war (such as the naïve American view that all other nations "should" be democracies). One can, by choice, reject the temptation to habitual judgmentalism. The result is a great inner peace.

June 7

Every advance that we make in our awareness benefits unseen multitudes and strengthens the next step for others to follow. Every act of kindness is noticed by the universe and is preserved forever.

June 8

Simple kindness to one's self and all that lives is the most powerful transformational force of all. It produces no backlash, has no downside, and never leads to loss or despair. It increases one's own true power without exacting any toll. But to reach maximum power, such kindness can permit *no* exceptions, nor can it be practiced with the expectation of some selfish reward. And its effect is as far-reaching as it is subtle.

June 9

Humility removes the ego's underpinnings of judgmentalism, positionality, and moralizing.

June 10

Detachment from positionalities—and especially the positionalities occasioned by labeling—leads to serenity, freedom, and security. Greater serenity arises from relating to the context of life rather than to the content, which is primarily a game board of interacting egos. This broader style of relating to life leads to greater compassion and emancipation from being at the effect of the world.

June 11

Like any limiting ego position, it is not the position itself that requires relinquishment but the emotional payoff or energy that holding on to that position provides to the ego.

June 12

This moment is the only reality that is being experienced; all else is an abstraction and a mental construct. Therefore, one cannot actually live 70 years at all; only this exact, fleeting moment is possible.

June 13

Personal judgment is based on perception that is reinforced by belief and prior programming, all of which are held in place by the payoff of the negative energies of the ego. The ego just "loves" suffering a "wrong," being the martyr, being misunderstood, and being the endless victim of life's vicissitudes. Consequently, it gets an enormous payoff—not only from the positionality itself but also from sympathy, self-pity, entitlements, importance, or being "center stage" in which the self is the hero or heroine of the melodrama.

June 14

The world is actually entertainment. Like amusement, it is meant to be worn lightly. Heaven is within and is revealed by awareness. The world is merely an appearance. Its melodrama is an artifice of the distorted sense of perception. It leads one to think that the world is large, powerful, and permanent and that the Self is small, weak, and transitory; exactly the opposite is true.

June 15

The option for truth, peace, and joy is always available, although seemingly buried behind an ignorance and non-awareness that results from having chosen other options as a habit of thought. The inner truth reveals itself when all other options are refused by surrender to God.

June 16

By internal observation, one can differentiate that the personality is a system of learned responses and the persona is not the real "I"; the real "I" lies behind and beyond it. One is the witness of that personality, and there is no reason one has to identify with it at all.

June 17

The truly successful have no inclination to act arrogantly, for they consider themselves not better than others, just more fortunate. They see their position as a *stewardship,* a responsibility to exercise their influence for the greatest benefit of all.

June 18

At first, spiritual purification seems difficult, but eventually it becomes natural. To consistently choose love, peace, or forgiveness leads one out of the house of mirrors. The joy of God is so exquisite that any sacrifice is worth the effort and seeming pain.

June 19

Peace can be the consequence of surrender to the inevitabilities of life. The religious/spiritual skeptic can look within and observe that the inner fundamental irreducible quality of life is the capacity of awareness, consciousness, and the substrate of subjectivity.

Without consciousness, we would not "know" or even "know if we know," so that consciousness is the determinable awareness of existence, irrespective of the content of that existence. Thus, consciousness itself can be accepted as an obvious reality, without the elaboration of being Divine (as recommended by the Buddha). To "be" is one thing; to know that one "is" obviously requires a more transcendent quality.

June 20

To surrender a goal does not mean to automatically lose it. What is illusive via greed often effortlessly materializes as a consequence of evolving to a higher level of consciousness.

June 21

There is a peaceful relief when judgment and criticism are abandoned, since they cause constant unconscious guilt as well as fear of retribution.

June 22

One can ask oneself the question, *Is this worth giving up God for?* Thus, ego positionality has a price, which is where the willingness should be addressed. Each positionality is based on the presumption that its fulfillment will bring happiness. Thus, nothing is really valued aside from the illusion that it will bring that about.

June 23

Without belief in its appearance as defined by perception, the world we thought was real disappears. When one chooses to be at one with the inner, ever-present potentiality of joy and peace, the world transforms into a humorous amusement park; and all the drama is seen to be just drama.

June 24

Existence is its own reward. It is more gratifying in the long term to fulfill potentiality than to try to achieve results. Therefore, one becomes aligned with excellence of performance for its own sake.

June 25

Rational humility, through which the mind becomes teachable, is basic to learning. The mind can then absorb, incorporate, and identify with verifiable and true knowledge. The key to success is to study and imitate a truthful authority rather than resist or attack it through competitive envy, jealousy, or hostility.

June 26

The higher the level of consciousness, the greater the likelihood that what is held in mind will actualize. Thus, to see solutions that "serve the highest goal" is more powerful than simply projecting fulfillment of merely personal selfish desires and gain.

June 27

Partial and limited positionalities create the illusions called "problems." In reality, no such thing as a problem is possible; there is merely what we want and what we don't want. Suffering is due to resistance.

June 28

One "owes" contrition and confession only to the Self. One "owes" the undoing of "sin and guilt" to the Self. One "owes" the obligation to change one's ways to the Self. One "owes" it to the Self to give up positionalities. Suffering only serves the ego. Of what use would it be to God, Who has no needs or emotion, and Who would in no way be pleasured by human agony?

June 29

A helpful source of strength during the processing out of painful emotions is to identify with all humanity and realize that suffering is universal and innate to the phenomenon of being human and the evolution of the ego.

June 30

Success in any venture is simply the automatic consequence of being the best that one can be as a lifestyle, without looking for gain.

July 1

The linear domain entails suffering; thus, the best Teachers throughout history taught the ways of salvation or enlightenment as the only answer to escape from that suffering.

July 2

Accept that all sentient beings live by faith. Despite naïve and pretentious claims to the contrary, all people live solely by the principle of faith—it is only a question of faith in *what*. Faith can be placed in the illusory, the intellect, reason, science, progress, political and worldly power, ego satisfactions, pleasure, wealth, or hope (such as "tomorrow").

July 3

Dedication is a more important sign of integrity than enthusiasm. It is necessary to have faith in a pathway and clear away doubts to ascertain if they are realistic or merely forms of resistance. A seeker should have the security and support of inner certainty and firm conviction that are consequent to study, personal research, and investigation. Thus, a pathway should be intrinsically reconfirming by discovery and inner experience. A true pathway unfolds, is self-revelatory, and is subject to reconfirmation experientially.

July 4

Simply stated, integrity is strong, "works," and is constructive and successful, whereas its opposite fails. Integrity is therefore practical; its absence leads to weakness and collapse.

July 5

By being loving toward others, we discover that we are surrounded by love and lovingness. When we unreservedly support life without expecting gain, life supports us in return. Whenever we abandon gain as a motive, life responds with unexpected generosity. And when we perceive in this way, the miraculous begins to appear in the life of every dedicated spiritual aspirant.

July 6

The more educated spiritual seeker takes responsibility for what seems to be happening "out there," since inner investigation always reveals that the perception and source of the "out there" is actually "in here."

July 7

There is no opposite to the Allness, Love, and Totality of God. Unless one is unreservedly willing to surrender one's very life and die for God, then spiritual purification should be the goal of one's endeavor instead of enlightenment.

July 8

Problems cannot be solved at their own calibrated level of consciousness, but only by rising to the next higher level.

July 9

An individual's level of consciousness is determined by the principles to which he or she is committed. To maintain progress in consciousness, there can be no wavering from principle, or the individual will fall back to a lower level.

July 10

In reality, it is the forgiver and not the forgiven who benefits most.

July 11

The narcissistic core of the ego is aligned with being "right," whether being "right" means being in agreement with wisdom or rejecting it as invalid. With humility, the serious searcher discovers that the mind alone, despite its education, is unable to resolve the dilemma of how to ascertain and validate truth, which would require confirmation by subjective experience as well as objective, provable criteria.

July 12

Q: *The attractions of the world seem endless. Is it really safe to go there? I often just want to escape.*

A: The attractions are not innate to the world, but reflect projected values and the expectation of the payoffs of ego satisfactions. In actuality, joy stems from within and is not dependent on externals. Pleasure is associated with what is valued and esteemed. Much of projected value arises from imagination, and values reflect desires. In reality, nothing is more valuable than anything else other than spiritual fulfillment.

July 13

When one willingly lets a hated perpetrator "off the hook" by forgiveness, it is not that person who is taken off the hook, but oneself.

July 14

To choose to forgive by giving up the "juice" of justified resentments and grudges disconnects all the associated thoughts and grievances from them, along with their multiple rationalizations and memories.

July 15

The ego is clever. It substitutes spiritual pride for personal pride. It goes right on, undaunted. It takes personal credit for spiritual comprehension instead of realizing that the capacity for understanding itself is a spiritual gift from God.

July 16

Q: What prayers are useful?

A: Ask to be the servant of the Lord, a vehicle of Divine love, a channel of God's will. Ask for direction and Divine assistance, and surrender all personal will through devotion. Dedicate one's life to the service of God. Choose love and peace above all other options. Commit to the goal of unconditional love and compassion for all life, in all its expressions, and surrender all judgment to God.

July 17

Supplication and prayer to Divinity are facilitated by a profound and deep surrender to humility. This humility is merely the truthful acknowledgment of the actual fact that the ego/mind, by virtue of its structure and design, is intrinsically incapable of being able to differentiate truth from falsehood (that is, essence from appearance).

July 18

Courage implies the willingness to try new things and to deal with the vicissitudes of life. At this level of empowerment, one is able to cope with and effectively handle the opportunities of life. . . . There is the capacity to face fears or character defects and to grow despite them, and anxiety does not cripple endeavor as it does at the lower stages of evolution.

July 19

Courage does not mean absence of fear, but the willingness to surmount it—which, when accomplished, reveals hidden strength and the capacity for fortitude. Fear of failure is diminished by realizing that one is responsible for the intention and effort but not the result, which is dependent on many other conditions and factors that are nonpersonal.

July 20

At every instant, one is really making a choice between heaven or hell. The cumulative effect of all these choices determines the calibrated level of consciousness and one's karmic and spiritual fate.

July 21

Q: Is the ego the source of karma?

A: It is its locus and repository. It is very important to realize that the ego and karma are one and the same thing.

July 22

The capacity for forgiveness arises from accepting with honest humility the limitations inherent in the human condition itself—which is, after all, merely on a learning curve of the evolution of consciousness.

July 23

Compassion arises from the acceptance of human limitation and by seeing that everyone is really the captive of his or her own worldview. With nonattachment, there is no longer the pressure to try to change the world or other people's viewpoints, or to make them wrong by virtue of disagreement.

July 24

The difficulty with a closed mind is that it is innately prideful.

July 25

If unimpeded, the human psyche is creative and inventive. Each level of consciousness has its own innate problems, but also its concordant solutions. The desire to undo the past is understandable but futile, and blinds one to the opportunities of the present.

July 26

The mature mind knows that it is evolving and that growth and development are satisfying and pleasurable in and of themselves. Maturity implies that one has learned how to be comfortable with uncertainty and has included it as a legitimate ingredient. Uncertainty leads to discovery, whereas skepticism is stultifying.

July 27

The downside of pride is arrogance and denial. These characteristics block growth.

July 28

The evolution is to turn one's life into a prayer/contemplation/meditation/supplication and surrender. One's life becomes the prayer—the prayer is the contemplation.

July 29

Every act of kindness, consideration, forgiveness, or love affects everyone.

July 30

Our perception of events happening in time is analogous to a traveler watching the landscape unfold before him. But to say that the landscape unfolds before the traveler is merely a figure of speech: Nothing is actually unfolding; nothing is actually becoming manifest. There's only the progression of awareness.

July 31

The ego/mind presumes and is convinced that its perceptions and interpretations of life experiences are the "real" thing and therefore "true." It also believes by projection that other people see, think, and feel the same way; and if they do not, they are mistaken and therefore wrong. Thus, perception reinforces its hold by reification and presumptions.

August 1

Q: *How should one best relate to the world?*

A: To be "in" it but not "of" it. Remember that the world is a means and not an end. Nonattached interaction reveals habitual styles and attitudes that are consequent to inner ego positionalities.

August 2

Meaning is so important that when life loses meaning, suicide commonly ensues. When life loses meaning, we first go into depression; when life becomes sufficiently meaningless, we leave it altogether. Force has transient goals; when those goals are reached, the emptiness of meaninglessness remains. Power, on the other hand, motivates us endlessly. If our lives are dedicated, for instance, to enhancing the welfare of everyone we contact, our lives can never lose meaning.

August 3

If we examine much of what the world traditionally calls "evil," what we discover is not evil, which is an abstraction, epithet, and label. Instead, we see behaviors that could be described as primitive, infantile, egotistical, narcissistic, selfish, and ignorant, complicated by the psychological mechanisms of denial, projection, and paranoia in order to justify hatred.

August 4

Pride in the form of the vanity of thoughts, concepts, and opinions are all the basis of ignorance. The antidote is radical humility, which undoes the domination of perception. Ask for truth to be revealed instead of assuming that you already know it.

August 5

The most important quality necessary for true growth and evolution is the practice and principle of humility. It is far less painful to voluntarily adopt a fundamental attitude of humility than to have it thrust upon oneself as the painful consequence of ineptitude. Despite its negative public and social image in some quarters of society, humility is indicative of expertise, wisdom, and maturity. Because truth is the very bedrock and ultimate reality upon which humility is based, it is not a vulnerability in and of itself. Rather, humility reveals that the mind can only "know about," and that it cannot differentiate between appearance and essence.

August 6

The ego relies on force; the spirit influences by power. Awareness knows that it is not what you do, but who you are and what you have become, that counts in the long run.

August 7

I, of myself, really know nothing is factual, for at best, the mind has only impressions and presumptions. Life "makes sense" solely in retrospect.

August 8

Humor is a means of detachment or recontextualizing the events of life. It is a way of being lighthearted and "wearing the world like a loose garment." It leads to compassion for the totality of human life and reveals the option that one can play at life without getting involved in it as though it were an exhausting life-and-death struggle.

August 9

Humor is important to the maturation process, whereby we learn how to not take ourselves so seriously and to laugh at ourselves, thus decreasing narcissistic defensiveness. To be prone to "hurt feelings" is egocentric and a form of social paranoia. When we admit our downside and learn to laugh at it, we are no longer vulnerable to slights and insults.

August 10

Malice literally makes us sick; we are always the victims of our own vindictiveness. Even secret hostile thoughts result in a physiological attack on one's own body.

August 11

Spiritual teachings need to be accepted to become integrated. Resistance comes from the ego, which lacks humility and which, out of pride, resents being "wrong." It is better to realize that one is not giving up wrong views but is instead adopting better ones.

August 12

The wise know that the intellect can take one only so far, and beyond that, faith and belief must substitute for knowledge.

August 13

The spiritual information necessary for advanced states should be learned early and stored away for when it is needed. The possible downside of hearing advanced information early is the intellect's presumption of the prideful *I know that.* It is better to hold the information as *I have heard that.* To truly "know" is to "be," at which point one does not know; instead, one is.

August 14

Most humans believe that love is something you get, that it is an emotion, that it has to be deserved, and that the more they give away, the less they will have. The opposite is the truth. Lovingness is an attitude that transforms one's experience of the world. We become grateful for what we have instead of being prideful. We express our lovingness when we acknowledge others and their contributions to life and to our conveniences. Love is not an emotion, but a way of being and relating to the world.

August 15

Love is misunderstood to be an emotion; actually, it is a state of awareness, a way of being in the world, a way of seeing oneself and others. Love for God or nature or even one's pets opens the door to spiritual inspiration. The desire to make others happy overrides selfishness. The more we give love, the greater our capacity to do so becomes. It is a good beginning practice to merely mentally wish others well throughout the course of the day. Love blossoms into lovingness, which becomes progressively more intense, nonselective, and joyful.

August 16

One has to see through the mind's illusion that it knows any- thing. This is called "humility" and has the value of opening the door for realizations, revelations, and intuitive knowingness.

August 17

Strong intention plus dedication assisted by inspiration can surprisingly bring success, despite prior failures. This reveals the inner capacity for bravery and fortitude that greatly increases self-esteem and confidence. Many of life's travails can only be traversed by "white-knuckling it," which builds self-confidence.

August 18

The antidote to pride is to choose humility and integrity instead of a positionality such as being important or right, getting even, indulging in blame, or seeking admiration. All credit for accomplishment is given to God as the presence of the Divinity within instead of to the ego; therefore, accomplishment results in gratitude and joy rather than vulnerable pridefulness.

August 19

Courage arises from commitment and integrity of alignment and dedication. A valuable characteristic of dedication is felicity, which eventually becomes empowered as a quiet but persistent inner fervor. The value of watchful witnessing is that even just awareness of an ego defect tends to undo it. By surrender and prayerful invocation, Divine Will facilitates transition from the lesser to the greater, for the Self effortlessly supports and energizes intention.

The Self is like a magnetic attraction by which the personal will is progressively surrendered and resistance is weakened. Thus, the pathway itself is self-fulfilling and gratifying, and reveals progressive rewards. Each step, no matter how seemingly small, is equally valuable.

August 20

Love is the leading edge of reality and the oneness and essence of the spirit. To deny love is to deny God.

August 21

Lovingness is a way of relating to the world. It is a generosity of attitude that expresses itself in seemingly small but powerful ways. It is a wish to bring happiness to others, to brighten their day and lighten their load. To merely be friendly and complimentary to everyone one meets in the course of a day is revealing.

August 22

When one's attitude toward everything becomes a devotion, Divinity reveals itself.

August 23

Through compassion arises the desire to understand rather than condemn.

August 24

A source of regret and loss is the unrealistic expectations of the self and others. Nothing in the world of form is permanent. Eventually, all has to be surrendered to the will of God. To succeed at surrendering, it is necessary to realize that God's will is not personalized to suit individual wishes. The will of God is really the karmic design of the entire universe. To surrender to God's will is to surrender to the truth that nothing other than the Ultimate Reality is permanent. All that arises in form passes away. A loss is an opportunity to become freed from an attachment.

August 25

The spiritually evolved person who has few wants or attachments is relatively immune to grief, as the experience of the source of happiness originates from within and is not dependent on externals. If the source of happiness is acquired through ego mechanisms, it is based on imagery, belief systems, and projected values rather than on Absolute Reality itself, which is invulnerable to loss. Objects, qualities, or relationships become overvalued by virtue of the mechanism of attachment and the ensuing projection of value.

August 26

To sincerely dedicate oneself to be a servant of the Lord and ask what is His will is sufficient. The answers reveal themselves without necessarily even having to be formulated. To be "spiritual" simply means an intention.

August 27

One must remember that love and peace are the greatest threats to the ego, which defends itself by resorting to entrenched positionalities that lie hidden in the unconscious.

August 28

Love is the opportunity to surrender the personal will to God and to reassess what is the overall purpose of the gift of human life.

August 29

Humility is not just an attitude, but also a reality based on facts. With inner honesty, a devotee needs to realize the limitations inherent in just being human.

August 30

Spiritual purity is the consequence of self-honesty, which is a result of true devotion. To be a servant of God is to align with Divine guidance, which leads to looking to the Self rather than catering to the self or the world.

August 31

By virtue of devotion, there is alignment with inner integrity that results in the self-honesty and conviction necessary to transcend the seduction of transitory emotional payoffs of the intransigent ego.

September 1

Devotion is of the heart—for at times, it is solely via the power of the heart and Divine love that an obstacle can be transcended.

September 2

What the people in the world actually want is the recognition of who they really are on the highest level, to see that the same Self radiates forth within everyone, heals their feeling of separation, and brings about a feeling of peace.

September 3

Peace is absolutely a choice and a decision, although not a popular one in our society, despite all the rhetoric about the term. The decision to overlook the seeming inequities of life instead of reacting to them is certainly a choice.

September 4

The true source of joy and happiness is the realization of one's existence in this very moment. The source of pleasure always comes from within, even though it is occasioned by some external event or acquisition. In any one instant of time, no such thing as a problem can exist. Unhappiness arises from going beyond the reality of the now and creating a story out of the past or the future—which, because neither exists, has no reality.

September 5

Joy arises from within each moment of existence rather than from any outer source.

September 6

Inner peace results from surrender of either attractions or aversions. Perceived values are primarily projections of "wants" and "not wants." The fewer the "wants," the greater the ease and satisfaction of life.

September 7

Fear itself actually precludes the awareness of the presence of God. Only when it is abandoned does profound surrender of the resistant ego reveal a peace beyond understanding.

September 8

Power comes from integrity and accepting responsibility for the consequences of one's own actions, choices, and decisions. All choices have inherent risks, and to pretend otherwise lacks integrity; in fact, it is game playing for gain.

September 9

One mechanism the ego uses to protect itself is to disown any painful data and project it onto the world and others.

September 10

By committing to inner honesty, it will become apparent that the underpinning of the ego's responses is the pleasure that is derived from them. There is an inner satisfaction that is the payoff of self-pity, anger, rage, hate, pride, guilt, fear, and the like. This inner pleasure, as morbid as it may sound, energizes and propagates all these emotions. To undo their influence, it is merely necessary to be willing to forego and surrender these questionable, inner secret pleasures to God and to look to God only for joy and happiness.

September 11

It takes inner discipline and surrender of attitudes not to fall into the temptation of identifying with a position about world events.

September 12

The events of the world trigger responses based on perception. It is a great theater that invites expressions of perceptions, illusions, and projections of positionalities. As such, one can either turn off the television and avoid it or see it as a major teaching tool.

September 13

Safeguards against being programmed by society are: (1) emotional detachment, in which all information is viewed as provisional; (2) awareness that ordinary mentalization is unable to discern perception from essence; and (3) knowing that the wolf often hides beneath sheep's clothing. This suspension of belief is the practical application of the basic dictum to "wear the world like a loose garment." To "be in the world but not of it" is a mode of attention that nevertheless still allows spontaneous interaction and function in society.

September 14

It is of little benefit to be personally self-critical or think that one "should" be farther along the road than one is. Spiritual evolution is irregular, and at times often seems sporadic and at other times stationary. Realize that guilt is a narcissistic indulgence.

September 15

Forgiveness is an extremely important major tool, especially when it is combined with the willingness of humility and acceptance of human fallibility and susceptibility to error. From spiritual intention, the surrendering of egoistic options may seem like a sacrifice—but when recontextualized, they are revealed to be a hidden gift.

September 16

Once one becomes willing to give love, the discovery quickly follows that one is surrounded by love and merely didn't know how to access it. Love is actually present everywhere, and its presence only needs to be realized.

September 17

Our experience of the world and life is totally the result of inner beliefs and positionalities. Out of love and respect for God arises the willingness to surrender all these prejudgments, and the humility that ensues opens the doors to the splendor of reality, which is the revelation of the Self. Love is the magic catalyst that brings about the awareness. In the end, faith is replaced by certainty, and therefore it is said that God is found by those who seek Him.

September 18

Consciousness research confirms that death is not a possibility. Life itself is supported by its eternal source, from which it cannot be separated. That which is linear, circumscribed, and limited in time comes into existence because of what is eternal and nonlinear.

September 19

Underlying all fears is the primordial, instinctual fear of death itself; therefore, much inner work can be bypassed by de-energizing this fear as early as possible in one's spiritual work. The fear of physical death arises from the animal instinct plus the narcissism of the ego, which is in love with itself. Death implies an end of experiencing, and experiencing is equated with life; thus, the ego clings to that which is linear and familiar.

September 20

The presence of God as love is self-revealing, since the duality of perception ceases as a consequence of surrendering positionalities. Love is therefore the doorway between the linear and the nonlinear domains. It is the grand avenue to the discovery of God.

September 21

If one looks at the feeling of happiness, it becomes clear that it is in fact located within. Although the trigger may appear to come from outside oneself, the sensation is totally an inner feeling of pleasure. The source of happiness is within, and it is released under favorable circumstances when the mind experiences a desired outcome. Through inner examination, one will discover that the event merely triggers an innate capacity. With the discovery that the source of happiness is actually within one's inner self and therefore cannot be lost, there is a reduction of fear.

September 22

To choose the love *for* God activates the love *of* God by prayer and worship.

September 23

What the world ignores as a weed is of beauty equal to that of the flower. The living-sculpture design of all nature is equal, without classification, and everything is realized to be of the same merit or worth. All is an expression of Divinity as creation—all is equally sacred and holy.

September 24

To the spiritual aspirant, desire and attachments are deterrents to progress, and as they arise, what they symbolize can be surrendered to God.

September 25

An illusion that drives desire and craving is that the object of desire has become imbued with an exaggerated importance and significance, resulting in an inflated value and attractiveness. Once the object has been acquired, it loses its magical aura, and that seductive image is now projected onto the next object of desire.

September 26

The discovery of the presence of God is not due to fear but to the surrender that was precipitated by the fear.

September 27

Attachment is the process whereby the suffering of loss occurs, irrespective of what the attachment is to or about: whether internal or external; whether object, relationship, social quality, or aspects of physical life. The ego perpetuates itself through its elaborate network of values, belief systems, and programs. Needs thus arise that gain more energy as they become embellished and elaborated, sometimes to the point of fixation.

The source of pain is not the belief system itself but one's attachment to it and the inflation of its imaginary value. The inner processing of attachments is dependent on the exercise of the will, which alone has the power to undo the mechanism of attachment by the process of surrender. This may be subjectively experienced or contextualized as sacrifice, although it is actually a liberation. The emotional pain of loss arises from the attachment itself and not from the "what" that has been lost.

September 28

The world and everything in it is transitory; therefore, to cling to it brings suffering.

September 29

Temptation, seduction, desirability, and allure are all projections having to do with appearance and presumptions. These are associated with programmed fantasies of gain. Satisfaction of projected values constitutes the world of illusion.

September 30

Meaning is defined by context, which determines motive, and it is the motive that establishes spiritual value. To dedicate one's actions as a service of love to life is to sanctify them and transform them from self-seeking motives to unselfish gifts. We define excellence as dedication to the highest standards. Every act can then be held as an opportunity to glorify God by sheer purity of endeavor. All physical tasks and labor can be ingredients in one's contribution to the world. Even the smallest task can be seen as serving the common good and, if viewed in that light, work becomes ennobled.

October 1

Conflict exists in the mind of the observer and not in that which is observed.

October 2

How life is contextualized can bring either joy or resentment; stinginess can be replaced by generosity. If others benefit from one's efforts, so much the better. Everyone has the opportunity to contribute to harmony and beauty by kindness to others and thereby support the human spirit. That which is freely given to life flows back to us because we are equally part of that life. Like ripples on the water, every gift returns to the giver. What we affirm in others, we actually affirm in ourselves.

October 3

Remember that allegiance is due only to God, to one's relationship with Him, and to purity and holiness. No organization has any special favor with God, and all organizations as such are based on ego premises and illusions.

October 4

It is to be emphasized that that which is truly holy and of God brings only peace and love.

October 5

If the desire arises to surrender all obstacles to love and to God, then God is already present in the form of willingness. When one reaches devotion, there is already quite an advanced presence that is dissolving the ego and illuminating the way. Spiritual progress and discovery are accompanied by joy, which is the radiance of the Self, and quickly replaces the surrendered ego's positionalities. Spiritual inspiration increases in intensity each step along the way. When the self stops looking to the world or to the ego, it discovers that its source has been the Self all along.

October 6

The limitations of love have to do with perceived qualities and differences. Through inner self-honesty and examination, these areas of limitation are revealed, usually as residual judgments or as the impact from prior experience. A key to making love unconditional is the willingness of forgiveness to undo past reservations or experiences, or viewing people as unlovable.

October 7

The source of resistance to spiritual endeavor is the narcissistic core of the ego itself, which secretly claims sovereignty and authorship of one's existence, decisions, and actions. Thus, despite one's best efforts, willfulness and desire for gain or control have continued to erupt repetitiously.

This pattern can be diminished simply by accepting that it is natural for the ego to be vain, greedy, hateful, prideful, resentful, envious, and more. These were learned accretions to the ego during its evolutionary development over eons of time. Therefore, it is not necessary to feel guilty because these primitive emotions merely need to be outgrown and discarded in the transition from self-interest to Self-interest.

October 8

What needs to be surrendered are not the objects of desire, but the quality of desiring and the imbuing of the objects with the magical inflation of value.

October 9

It is only necessary to shift from devotion to the world to devotion to God and the spirit.

October 10

Like matter and energy, life cannot be destroyed but can only change form. Thus, death is actually only the leaving of the body. The sense of identity is, however, unbroken. The state of "me" (self) is constant and continues after it separates from the physical expiration; that is, there has to be a "who" that goes on to heaven or other realms or chooses to reincarnate.

October 11

Excessive desire creates the illusion of lack, just like seeming money problems are created by spending faster than income.

October 12

The essential fundamental principles for spiritual endeavor are the time-honored ones, such as devotion, humility, fortitude, willingness to surrender, and faith and trust in God. These are reinforced by dedication, prayer, and the supplication and invocation of God's Grace by an act of the spiritual will. . . . These are empowered by intention, which results in alignment and integration whereby the basic principles become operative. Devotion is a consequence of assent by the will. Complete and total surrender to God can eclipse the process at any given point along the way.

October 13

To align one's life with spiritual intention expands its meaning and significance. While the ego/body/mind's life span is limited and temporary, the life of the spirit is eternal, and its importance thus eclipses transitory gains of ego satisfaction. The lesser is then surrendered to the greater by alignment, commitment, and agreement—because it is freely chosen rather than imposed, there is a lessening of resistance.

October 14

As we get closer to the discovery of the source of the ego's tenacity, we make the amazing critical discovery that *we are enamored with ourselves.*

October 15

The ego clings to emotionality, which is intimately connected with its positionalities; it pretends to think that it has no other choices. To "surrender to God" means to stop looking to the ego for solace and thrills and to discover the endless, serene joy of peace. To look within is to find the underlying, ever-present source of the illumination of the mind itself.

October 16

As the true source of happiness stems from within, desire cannot be satisfied—it is a constant projection of specialness onto the external, and is thus the pursuit of a fantasy. As one desire becomes fulfilled and satisfied, the focus then moves on to the next object of desire in an endless procession, like a carrot on a stick.

October 17

The common element of most fears is that they are based on the illusion that happiness is dependent on externals and therefore vulnerable. To overcome the illusion of vulnerability brings great relief and the correction of being run by fear. Life becomes benign and filled with satisfaction and an easygoing, confident attitude, instead of constant guardedness.

October 18

To undo shame, it is helpful to realize that it is based on pride. The loss of status is painful to the degree that the ego relies on pride as a prop to self-esteem. Were it not for narcissistic pride, a mistake or negative feedback would be experienced only as a regret and ascribed to human frailty and fallibility. Mistakes help one retain humility.

October 19

All forms of loss are a confrontation to the ego and its survival mechanisms. All aspects of human life are transient, so to cling to any aspect eventually brings grief and loss. Each incident, however, is an opportunity to search within for the source of life, which is ever present, unchanging, and not subject to loss or the ravages of time.

October 20

Relief of guilt and greater compassion for oneself and others occurs through realizing that the individual person did not volitionally create the structure of the ego, nor did anybody else. The human condition is primarily a karmic "given"—it can be accepted compassionately as such without condemnation, and is therefore neither good nor bad. Mankind lives in the realm of tension between emotional instincts and the counterbalancing power of spiritual awakening (that is, the animal/angel conflict).

October 21

There is no indication from any source of higher truth that God is influenced or assuaged by guilt. The great sages of history do not speak of guilt but instead refer to "sin" as being due to ignorance.

October 22

In the reality of nonduality, there is neither privilege nor gain nor loss nor rank. Just like a cork in the sea, each spirit rises or falls to its own level in the sea of consciousness by virtue of its own choices, not by any external force or favor. Some are attracted by the light and some seek the darkness, but it all occurs of its own nature by virtue of Divine freedom and equality.

October 23

There is absolutely nothing in ordinary human experience to compare with the joy of the presence of the love of God. No sacrifice is too great nor effort too much in order to realize that presence.

October 24

To understand the nature of God, it is necessary only to know the nature of love itself. To truly know love is to know and understand God, and to know God is to understand love.

October 25

To know that the Self is context—and, in contrast, the self is content—is already a huge leap forward. The naïve seeker merely keeps reshuffling the content.

October 26

The Self is like a person's inner grandmother who watches over him so he does not forget to take his raincoat or mail the rent check. God is not ominous but loving; fear arises from the imagination.

October 27

The innate qualities of Divinity are mercy and compassion. There are no favors to be sought. It is only necessary to accept what already exists as a given.

October 28

One makes a gift of one's life and endeavors by sanctifying them with love, devotion, and selfless service. That is the way of the heart to God. In that way, domestic life becomes a form of worship and the source of joy to all. When one seeks to uplift others, everyone is uplifted in the process. Giving is therefore self-rewarding, for there is actually no "other" that is being given to. Every kind thought or smile is therefore spiritual and benefits oneself as well as all the world.

October 29

Spiritual devotion is a continuous inner lifestyle that incorporates constant watchful awareness. External occurrences are transitory, whereas inner qualities of consciousness are more permanent. Inner work is a constant learning process whereby there is pleasure and satisfaction in discovery and the unfolding of insight.

October 30

Cessation of fear is the result of learning that the source of happiness is within. It stems from recognizing that this source is the joy of one's own existence, which is continuous and not dependent on externals. This results from surrendering expectations and demands on one's self, the world, and others. The thought *I can only be happy if I win or get what I want* is a guarantee of worry, anxiety, and unhappiness.

October 31

Fears are eliminated by graceful acceptance of the qualities inherent in the human condition, which brings to awareness the comforting realization that one's discomforts are shared equally by all. This results in a healing compassion toward all life. To become loving brings an end to the fear of loss of love, for lovingness engenders love wherever it goes.

November 1

All that is truly of God brings peace, harmony, and love, and is devoid of all forms of negativity. A spiritually aware person realizes that he or she can only carry the message, for it is the inner truth that is the teacher.

November 2

Divinity knows its own; therefore, to accept that truth is to already feel joy. To not experience joy by understanding this means that it is being resisted.

November 3

Enlightenment is not a condition to be obtained; it is merely a certainty to be surrendered to, for the Self is already one's Reality. It is the Self that is attracting one to spiritual information.

November 4

In Reality, there are no events; there are no beginnings or endings. The backdrop is silent, still, and undisturbed by the movie. One's reality is the context and not the content. The oneness of life appears to perception as multitudinous. What makes the appearances of the world seem real is a projection of the radiance of the Self. The movie itself has no intrinsic reality as perceived. The actual locus of the sense of realness lies totally within consciousness as subjectivity. Even if there were such a thing as an independent, objective reality, it would only be knowable because of one's internal subjectivity.

November 5

The radical Reality is that to understand the essence of anything is to know God.

November 6

Complete surrender to God unveils the truth; nothing is hidden. Only the ego is blind, and Reality lies just beyond the mind. Out of the fear of becoming nothing, consciousness denies its only reality that it is everything—the infinite, everlasting Allness out of which existence itself arises.

November 7

Realization is not a "gain" or an accomplishment, nor is it something that is "given" as a reward for being good. These are all notions from childhood. God is immutable and cannot be manipulated into granting favors or seduced by bargaining or adulation. Worship benefits the worshipper by reinforcing commitment and inspiration. God is still, silent, and unmoving.

November 8

Realize that if you *are* something, there is nothing to understand about it. Reality is the ultimate in simplicity.

November 9

The development of a spiritual ego can be avoided by the realization that spiritual progress is the result of God's Grace, not the result of one's personal endeavors.

November 10

The ego often seems to collapse in a piecemeal fashion. Once faith in the reality of the ego as being the true self is undermined, its dissolution has already begun. When one's loyalty and allegiance is shifted from the ego to the ultimate reality of God, a space is created. Into the opening flows God's Grace as represented by the Holy Spirit.

November 11

It is well to keep in mind at all times that the ego/mind does not experience the world but only its own perception of it.

November 12

The ego gets a grim pleasure and satisfaction from suffering and all the dishonest levels of pride, anger, desire, guilt, shame, and grief. The secret pleasure of suffering is addictive. Many people devote their entire lives to it and encourage others to follow suit. To stop this mechanism, the pleasure of the payoff has to be identified and willingly surrendered to God. Out of shame, the ego blocks out conscious awareness of its machinations, especially the secretiveness of the game of "victim."

November 13

We change the world not by what we say or do, but as a consequence of what we have become. Thus, every spiritual aspirant serves the world.

November 14

The way out of conflict is not to try to eliminate the negative, but instead to choose and adopt the positive. When one views that one's mission in life is to understand rather than to judge, this automatically resolves moral dilemmas.

November 15

Everyone is exposed to life in its expression as nature, as well as in that human interaction called society. Such interaction is impersonal, and the vicissitudes of life are inevitable and unavoidable—this can be either challenging or depressing, depending solely on one's point of view. Without positionalities, life is experienced as serene and interesting. This point of view fosters growth and (hopefully) wisdom, rather than self-pity or bitterness. Everyone is free to make a choice. The rain does not determine whether one will be happy or disappointed. The surrender of willfulness/positionality brings peace in all circumstances.

November 16

To endeavor to evolve spiritually is the greatest gift one can give. It actually uplifts all mankind from within because of the nature of power itself. Power radiates and is shared; whereas force is limited, self-defeating, and evanescent. All society is subliminally and subtly influenced by every kind and loving thought, word, or deed. Every forgiveness is a benefit to everyone. The universe notes and records every action and returns it in kind. Karma is actually the very nature of the universe because of the innate structure and function of the universe itself. In the universe, time is measured in eons. Beyond that, it doesn't even exist at all. Every kindness is therefore forever.

November 17

This process of spirituality, in which one works through the obstacles, may seem painful at times, but it is only transitional. The mistakes now reappear and are recontextualized from a higher understanding. This process is shortened and less painful if it is realized that habitual responses are not truly personal, but are part and parcel of the inheritance of being human.

November 18

The source of joy of spiritual endeavor stems from the work itself and is not dependent on outcomes or the achievement of goals. Each movement forward has an inner delight. There is, for instance, an inner pleasure that accompanies progress. The replacement of resentment with peaceful acceptance is its own reward. There is a progressive alteration in one's view of self and others. When this happens, one's own life story can then be reinterpreted from a more compassionate understanding.

November 19

The average person's psyche is overwhelmed by layers of pro-grammed belief systems of which they are unaware. Out of naïveté and the belief in the principles of causality, the supposed causes and their solutions are sought "out there." With maturity and the wisdom of spirituality, the search becomes directed inwardly, where the source and resolution are finally discovered.

November 20

To spiritualize one's life, it is necessary only to shift one's motive. To constantly be aware of one's actual motive tends to bring up positionality and pairs of opposites, such as gain versus service or love versus greed. These then become visible and are available for spiritual work because one is now conscious of them.

November 21

Spiritual reality is a greater source of pleasure and satisfaction than the world can supply. It is endless and always available in the present instead of the future. It is actually more exciting because one learns to live on the crest of the current moment, instead of on the back of the wave (which is the past) or on the front of the wave (which is the future). There is greater freedom from living on the exciting knife-edge of the moment than being a prisoner of the past or having expectations of the future.

November 22

If the goal of life is to do the very best one can do at each unfolding moment of existence, then, through spiritual work, one has already escaped the primary cause of suffering. In the stop-frame of the radical present, there is no life story to react to or edit. With this "one-pointedness" of mind, it soon becomes obvious that everything merely "is as it is," without comment or adjectives.

November 23

There is no timetable or prescribed path to God. Although each person's route is unique, the terrain to be covered is relatively common to all. The work is to surmount and transcend the common human failings that are inherent in the structure of the human ego. One would like to think that one is personal, yet the ego itself is not personal—it was inherited along with becoming a human being. Details differ based on past karma.

November 24

When the mind stops talking, one *is* aware that one is life. One is immersed in it rather than being on the surface, talking about it. Paradoxically, this enables full participation. When egocentricity diminishes, the joy of freedom and the sheer flow of life sweep one into total surrender. One then stops reacting to life, so it can be enjoyed with serenity.

November 25

We honor that which we esteem in others as well as ourselves. Out of this, one honors one's own humanity and that of others and ends up honoring all of life in all its expressions by resignation to Divine Will. With surrender of the ego, the spirit becomes aware of the sanctity of existence.

November 26

Spiritual evolution occurs as the result of removing obstacles and not actually acquiring anything new. Devotion enables surrender of the mind's vanities and cherished illusions so that the mind progressively becomes more free and open to the light of Truth.

November 27

Just one instant in a very high state can completely change a person's orientation to life, as well as his goals and values. It can be said that the individual who was is no more, and a new person is born out of the experience. Through hard-won progress on a dedicated spiritual path, this is the very mechanism of spiritual evolution.

November 28

Experientially, guilt is an operational "reality" until the underpinnings of the ego are removed. Spiritual seekers are sometimes prone to look back critically on their past actions from their new-found spiritual position. All self-examination should be done with compassion, keeping in mind that past errors arose within a different context. The best resolution of guilt is to rededicate oneself to God and one's fellow man, and to the forgiveness of self and others.

November 29

Wallowing in guilt is feeding the ego and is an indulgence. Therefore, there has to be the willingness to surrender it.

November 30

As evolution expresses itself in gradations, some people will be farther along the road than others. When we see this simple fact, forgiveness and compassion replace anger, fear, hatred, or condemnation. The willingness to forgive others is reflected in our own capacity for self-forgiveness and acceptance.

December 1

Q: What is a workable goal?

A: To verify spiritual truth experientially and to *become it* rather than just conform to it. The process is an unfolding of discovery resulting in greater happiness and diminution of fear, guilt, and other negative emotions. The motive is inner development, evolution, and fulfillment of potential, which is independent of the external world. Life becomes progressive rather than just repetitive. All experience is of equal value and innately pleasurable so that life stops being an endless sequence of alternating pleasure and displeasure. With inner progress, context expands, resulting in greater awareness of significance and meaning—and, therefore, gratification of potential.

December 2

Human life offers the maximum opportunity for spiritual evolution. Perception sees personal as well as social/political/ideational conflicts as obstacles to peace and happiness. In contrast, the spiritual Self sees perfection in the very same world.

December 3

As the payoffs of the ego are refused and surrendered, its grip on the psyche lessens, and spiritual experience progresses as the residuals of doubt are progressively relinquished. As a consequence, belief is replaced by experiential knowledge; the depth and intensity of devotion increases and may eventually supersede and eclipse all other worldly activities and interests.

December 4

The basic purpose of spiritual work and dedication is to transcend the innate evolutionary limitations of the ego and thereby access and develop the nascent capacity of consciousness itself, which bypasses all the limitations of the ego/self. Truth then presents itself by virtue of Divine Grace. Divinity reveals Itself to those who call upon It in God's time. The pace of spiritual evolution can seem slow, but spiritual endeavor is never futile. Progress can become very sudden and very major in dimension and impact.

December 5

Spiritual evolution is a lifetime commitment and a way of life by which the world and all experience subserve spiritual intention. There is no greater calling than to choose to be a servant of God. With spiritual progress, each increment is of equal importance—for, analogously, it is only through the removal of a single brick that an entire wall collapses, and the seemingly impossible becomes possible.

December 6

Choose to be easygoing, benign, forgiving, compassionate, and unconditionally loving—toward all life, in all its expressions, without exception, including oneself. Focus on unselfish service and the giving of love, consideration, and respect to all creatures.

December 7

Value, from the ego's viewpoint, is an emotionalized mentalization, and Reality does not require mentalization. With humility, one can honestly state and witness that everything merely "is as it is," independent of projected worth. Its intrinsic "value" is that it "is"; that is, existence is complete within itself and is not needful of projected nominalization as "special." When the Divine Essence of All of Creation shines forth without obstruction, then the ego/mind goes silent in awe.

December 8

Reality needs no agreement. Reality is not an acquisition, but is instead a purely spontaneous, subjective realization when the positionalities of the dualistic ego are surrendered.

December 9

Appreciate that every step forward benefits everyone. One's spiritual dedication and work is a gift to life and the love of mankind.

December 10

In true spiritual endeavor, no actual sacrifices are necessary or expected. *Sacrifice* in ordinary terminology means loss or even painful loss. True sacrifice really means the letting go of the lesser for the greater, and is self-rewarding rather than depleting.

December 11

Devotion dissolves fear, doubt, and hesitation; and it clarifies uncertainty. Intention also becomes even stronger, as does trust in God. Then arises the inner decision to totally abandon oneself to God.

December 12

Truth prevails when falsity is surrendered. To do this, however, requires great dedication, courage, and faith, which are supplied by Divine inspiration in response to surrender. The trigger is the consent of Divine Will.

December 13

Great leaps in levels of consciousness are always preceded by surrender of the illusion that "I know."

December 14

The first illusion to surrender is the belief that there is such a thing as "mind." Experientially, one can only state that thoughts, feelings, images, and memories come into one's awareness in an endless progression. The word *mind* is therefore only a concept, as is the word *ego.*

December 15

Trust in the love, mercy, infinite wisdom, and compassion of Divinity, which sees through all human error, limitation, and frailty. Place faith and trust in the love of God, which is all-forgiving, and understand that condemnation and fear of judgment stem from the ego. Like the sun, the love of God shines equally on all. Avoid negative depictions (*jealous, angry, destructive, partial, favoring, vengeful, insecure, vulnerable, contractual,* and so forth) of God as an anthropomorphic projection.

December 16

Traditionally, the relinquishment of the ego's programs has been described as arduous and difficult, requiring many lifetimes to accomplish. On the contrary, a profound humility and the willingness to surrender all to God at great depth make it possible for the transition to occur in a split second. Thus, the pathway to enlightenment may be viewed as a slow process or a sudden one.

December 17

To consciously choose alignment with Divinity and truth is reempowering and shifts identity from the self to the Self, resulting in an increase in confidence, courage, and personal dignity rather than self-abasement or self-denigration. Total surrender brings peace; partial or conditional surrender bring lingering doubt.

December 18

Surrender of the personal will to the will (wisdom) of God (or Providence or Higher Power) signifies relinquishment of control. One can expect the ego to resist doing so, and it invents excuses, counterarguments, and multiple fears in order to maintain illusory control. The ego's positions are reinforced by pride as well as desire for specific results. Thus, to the ego, to step back and invite the intervention of Divinity seems like a loss; whereas, to the spirit, it is definitely a win.

December 19

Truth is recognized. It presents itself to a field of awareness that has been prepared in order to allow the presentation to reveal itself. Truth and enlightenment are not acquired or achieved. They are states or conditions that present themselves when the conditions are appropriate.

December 20

Imperfection exists only in the mind's thoughts. No imperfection exists in the world as it is.

December 21

Ignorance does not yield to attack, but it dissipates in the light, and nothing dissolves dishonesty faster than the simple act of revealing the truth. The only way to enhance one's power in the world is by increasing one's integrity, understanding, and capacity for compassion.

December 22

The absolute subjectivity of revealed truth precludes all considerations or uncertainties, which stem only from the ego. When the ego collapses, all argument ceases and is replaced by silence. Doubt *is* the ego.

December 23

The primary defect now is, as it always has been, that the design of the human mind renders it intrinsically incapable of being able to tell truth from falsehood. This single, most crucial of all inherited defects lies at the root of all human distress and calamity.

December 24

The person who has found inner peace can no longer be intimidated, controlled, manipulated, or programmed. In this state, one is invulnerable to the threats of the world and therefore has mastered life.

December 25

The energy field of love is innately gratifying in and of its own quality. It is discovered that love is available everywhere and that lovingness results in the return of love. Although love may start out as conditional, with spiritual intention it becomes a way of life and a way of relating to life in all its expressions.

December 26

Q: How can one facilitate progress?

A: That is a natural curiosity. Choice results in proclivities that become habitual mind-sets of attention. Within each moment are all of the necessary elements for realization. Look for essence rather than just appearance. Everything is perfect if seen as it really is. Everything is exactly the way it is "supposed to be," whether it is shiny and new or rusty and dusty.

Avoid adjectives, for they are all projected, mentalized qualifications. Later, you can even drop verbs and adverbs, for nothing is actually "doing" anything; it just innately *is*. Transition is a phenomenon that stems from within the observer, who sees sequence as a verb. If seen in less than 1/10,000th of a second, everything appears to be stationary.

December 27

All reactions to life are subjective. There is nothing happening that is awful, exciting, sad, good, or bad. It is pointless to hold a position that catastrophes shouldn't "happen" or that the innocent didn't deserve it, or isn't it awful, or it must be somebody's fault. With a broad view, one can remain unperturbed by either the content or the context of life. That requires giving up judgments, expectations, or sensitivities.

December 28

Persistent devotion to spiritual truth and love allows for the dissolution of resistances.

December 29

Surrender is a constant process of not resisting or clinging to the moment, but instead, continuously turning it over to God. The attention is thus focused on the process of letting go and not on the content of the "what" that is being surrendered.

December 30

The spirit and the heart are one. It is the heart that is at one with God, not the mind. To discover one's own heart is to discover God.

December 31

The truths learned have to be put into daily practice to be effective, and they exist beyond the words. If this is done, change takes place. The purpose of information is for it to be absorbed with familiarity and then mature into understanding.

GLOSSARY

This glossary is a composite of edited excerpts from Dr. Hawkins's work:

Consciousness: Consciousness is the irreducible substrate of the human capacity to know or experience, to perceive or witness, and it is the essence of the capacity for awareness itself. It is the formless, invisible field of energy of infinite dimension and potentiality, and the foundation of all existence. It is independent of time, space, or location, yet all-inclusive and all-present.

Consciousness is the unlimited, omnipresent, universal energy field, carrier wave, and reservoir of all information available in the universe—and, more important, it is the very essence and substrate of the capacity to know or experience. Even more critically, consciousness is the irreducible, primary quality of all existence.

Consciousness is an impersonal quality of Divinity expressed as awareness and is nondualistic and nonlinear. It is like infinite space that is capable of awareness and a quality of the Divine essence.

Context: The total field of observation predicated by a point of view.

Context includes any significant facts that qualify the meaning of a statement or event. Data is meaningless unless its context is defined. To "take out of context" is to distort the significance of a statement by failing to identify contributory accessory conditions that would qualify the inference of meaning.

Duality: The world of form characterized by seeming separation of objects, reflected in conceptual dichotomies such as "this/that," "here/there," "then/now," or "yours/mine." This perception of limitation is produced by the senses because of the restriction implicit in a fixed point of view.

Ego (or self with a small *s*): The ego is the imaginary doer behind thought and action. Its presence is firmly believed to be necessary and essential for survival. The reason is that the ego's primary quality is perception, and as such, it is limited by the paradigm of supposed causality. The ego could be called the central processing and planning center; the integrative, executive, strategic, and tactical focus that orchestrates, copes, sorts, stores, and retrieves. It can be thought of as a set of entrenched habits of thought that are the result of entrainment by invisible energy fields that dominate human consciousness. They become reinforced by repetition and by the consensus of society. Further reinforcement comes from language itself.

To think in language is a form of self-programming. The use of the prefix "I" as the subject, and therefore the implied cause of all actions, is the most serious error and automatically creates a duality of subject and object. Put another way, the ego is a set of programs in which reason operates through complex, multilayered series of algorithms wherein thought follows certain decision trees that are variously weighted by past experience, indoctrination, and social forces; it is therefore not a self-created condition. The instinctual drive is attached to the programs, thereby causing physiological processes to come into play.

Enlightenment: A state of unusual awareness that replaces ordinary consciousness. The self is replaced by the Self. The condition is beyond time or space, is silent, and presents itself as a revelation. The condition follows dissolution of the ego.

Karma: In essence, individual karma is an information package (analogous to a computer chip) that exists within the nonphysical domain of consciousness. It contains the code of stored information that is intrinsic to, and a portion of, the spiritual body or soul. The core represents a condensation of all past experiences, together with associated nuances of thought and feeling. The spirit body retains freedom of choice, but the range of choices has already been patterned.

Karma is linear, propagates via the soul, and is inherited as the consequence of significant acts of the will. Karma really means accountability—and, as cited in previous spiritual research, every entity is answerable to the universe. To summarize, as is commonly known, karma (spiritual fate) is the consequence of decisions of the will and determines spiritual destiny after physical death (the celestial levels, hell, purgatory, or the so-called inner astral planes [bardos]). Included also is the option of reincarnation in the human physical domain, which, by consciousness-calibration research, can only be done by agreement with the individual will. So all humans have, by agreement, chosen this pathway. In addition, consciousness research confirms that all persons are born under the most optimal conditions for spiritual evolution, no matter what the appearance seems to be.

Linear: Following a logical progression in the manner of Newtonian physics and, therefore, solvable by traditional mathematics through the use of differential equations.

Nonduality: When the limitation of a fixed locus of perception is transcended, there is no longer an illusion of separation nor of space and time as we know them. On the level of nonduality there is observing but no observer, as subject and object are one. You-and-I becomes the One Self experiencing all as Divine. In nonduality, consciousness experiences itself as both manifest and unmanifest, yet there is no experiencer. In this reality, the only thing that has a beginning and an ending is the act of perception itself.

Positionality: The positionalities are structures that set the entire thinking mechanism in motion and activate its content. Positionalities are programs, not the real Self. The world holds an endless array of positions that are arbitrary presumptions and totally erroneous. Primordial positionalities are: (1) *Ideas have significance and importance;* (2) *There is a dividing line between opposites;* (3) *There is a value of authorship—thoughts are valuable because they are "mine";* (4) *Thinking is necessary for control, and survival depends on control.* All positionalities are voluntary.

Self (capital *S*): The Self is beyond, yet innate in, all form—timeless, without beginning or end, changeless, permanent, and immortal. Out of it arises awareness, consciousness, and an infinite condition of "at home-ness." It is the ultimate subjectivity from which everyone's sense of "I" arises. The Infinite Reality does not even know itself as "I" but as the very substrate of the capacity for such a statement. It is invisible and all present. The Self is the Reality of reality, the Oneness and All-ness of Identity. It is the ultimate "I-ness" of consciousness itself as the manifestation of the unmanifest. Thus, only can the indescribable be described.

Subjectivity: Life is lived solely on the level of experience and none other. All experience is subjective and nonlinear; therefore, even the linear, perceptual, sequential delineation of "reality" cannot be experienced except subjectively. All "truth" is a subjective conclusion. All life in its essence is nonlinear, nonmeasurable, nondefinable. It is purely subjective.

Truth: Truth is relative and only "true" in a given context. All truth is only so within a certain level of consciousness. For instance, to forgive is commendable, but at a later stage, one sees there is actually nothing to forgive. There is no "other" to be forgiven. Everyone's ego is equally unreal, including one's own. Perception is not reality. Truth arises out of subjectivity and is obvious and self-revealing. Truth is radical subjectivity. With the collapse of the illusions of duality, including the supposed "reality" of a separate "self," there remains only the state of the Infinite "I," which is the manifestation of the Unmanifest as the Self. Truth has no opposites, such as falsity or "off-ness." Nothing is hidden from the field of consciousness. The ultimate truth is beyond is-ness, beingness, or any intransitive verb. Any attempt at Self-definition, such as "I Am That I Am"—or even just "I Am"—is redundant. The ultimate reality is beyond all names. "I" signifies the radical subjectivity of the state of Realization. It is in itself the complete statement of Reality.

ABOUT THE AUTHORS

David R. Hawkins, M.D., Ph.D., was Director of the Institute for Spiritual Research, Inc., and remains a widely known authority within the field of consciousness research even after his death in 2012. He wrote and taught from the unique perspective of an experienced clinician, scientist, and teacher, having been a life member of the American Psychiatric Association, with 50 years of clinical experience. His background and research is outlined in *Who's Who in America* and *Who's Who in the World*. He was honored worldwide with many titles, and had been knighted and honored in the East with the title "Tae Ryoung Sun Kak Tosa" (Foremost Teacher of the Way to Enlightenment). Dr. Hawkins lectured widely at universities (Harvard, Oxford, et al.) and also to spiritual groups from Westminster Abbey and Notre Dame to Catholic, Protestant, and Buddhist monasteries. His life was devoted to the upliftment of mankind.

Website: **www.veritaspub.com**

Scott Jeffrey is the author of numerous books, including *Creativity Revealed: Discovering the Source of Inspiration.* He has also written a biography of Dr. David Hawkins.

≋ NOTES ≋

≈ NOTES ≈

≈ NOTES ≈

Hay House Titles of Related Interest

YOU CAN HEAL YOUR LIFE, the movie, starring Louise Hay & Friends
(available as a 1-DVD program, an expanded 2-DVD set,
and an online streaming video)
Learn more at **www.hayhouse.com/louise-movie**

THE SHIFT, the movie, starring Dr. Wayne W. Dyer
(available as a 1-DVD program, an expanded 2-DVD set,
and an online streaming video)
Learn more at **www.hayhouse.com/the-shift-movie**

*A DAILY DOSE OF SANITY: A Five-Minute Soul
Recharge for Every Day of the Year,* by Alan Cohen

*DAILY OM: Inspirational Thoughts for a Happy,
Healthy, and Fulfilling Day,* by Madisyn Taylor

EVERYDAY POSITIVE THINKING, by Louise Hay and Friends

MANIFEST YOUR DESIRES: 365 Ways to Make Your Dreams a Reality,
by Esther and Jerry Hicks (The Teachings of Abraham®)

*SQUEEZE THE DAY: 365 Ways to bring JOY and
JUICE into Your Life,* by Loretta LaRoche

STAYING ON THE PATH, by Dr. Wayne W. Dyer

*VITAMINS FOR THE SOUL: Daily Doses of Wisdom
for Personal Empowerment,* by Sonia Choquette

All of the above are available at your local bookstore,
or may be ordered by contacting Hay House (see next page).

We hope you enjoyed this Hay House book. If you'd like to receive our online catalog featuring additional information on Hay House books and products, or if you'd like to find out more about the Hay Foundation, please contact:

Hay House, Inc., P.O. Box 5100, Carlsbad, CA 92018-5100
(760) 431-7695 or (800) 654-5126
(760) 431-6948 (fax) or (800) 650-5115 (fax)
www.hayhouse.com® • www.hayfoundation.org

———

Published in Australia by: Hay House Australia Pty. Ltd.,
18/36 Ralph St., Alexandria NSW 2015
Phone: 612-9669-4299 • *Fax:* 612-9669-4144
www.hayhouse.com.au

Published in the United Kingdom by: Hay House UK, Ltd.,
The Sixth Floor, Watson House, 54 Baker Street, London W1U 7BU
Phone: +44 (0)20 3927 7290 • *Fax:* +44 (0)20 3927 7291
www.hayhouse.co.uk

Published in India by: Hay House Publishers India,
Muskaan Complex, Plot No. 3, B-2, Vasant Kunj, New Delhi 110 070
Phone: 91-11-4176-1620 • *Fax:* 91-11-4176-1630
www.hayhouse.co.in

———

Access New Knowledge.
Anytime. Anywhere.

Learn and evolve at your own pace
with the world's leading experts.

www.hayhouseU.com